D1736928

Jennifer Clement

Also by Jennifer Clement

Poetry

The Next Stranger / El Próximo extraño
Newton's Sailor / El marinero de Newton
Lady of the Broom / La dama de la escoba

Non Fiction

Widow Basquiat

Fiction

A True Story Based on Lies
A Salamander-Child
The Poison That Fascinates
Prayers for the Stolen

JENNIFER CLEMENT

New and Selected Poems

Shearsman Books

Published in the United Kingdom in 2008 by
Shearsman Books Ltd
58 Velwell Road
EXETER
EX4 4LD

www.shearsman.com

ISBN 978-1-905700-46-2

ACKNOWLEDGEMENTS

Lady of the Broom was first published in 2002 in a bilingual edition in
Mexico by Editorial Aldus, Mexico City. *Newton's Sailor* and *The Next
Stranger* were first published in 1997 and 1993, respectively, in bilingual
editions by Ediciones El Tucán de Virginia, Mexico City. The poem 'Iceman'
previously appeared in the anthology *Cuerpo Erotico*, edited by Juan Gustavo
Cobo Borda (Villegas Editores, Colombia, 2005).

*The author wishes to thank the Sistema Nacional de Creadores de Arte from
Mexico's Fondo Nacional para la Cultura y las Artes for their assistance during
the writing of some of these poems.*

*La autora agradece al Sistema Nacional de Creadores de Arte del Fondo
Nacional para la Cultura y las Artes de México por el apoyo recibido durante la
creación de una parte de esta obra.*

Contents

New Poems

Iceman	11
The Dream	13
Deus Ex Machina	14
Scarecrow	16
Making Love in Spanish	18
Swimming	19
The Ocean House	20
The Night House	22
I Wrote it for You	23
Heart Poem	25
Woodsman	28

Lady of the Broom	31

from Newton's Sailor

Far from the Smoked Glass	63
Einstein Explains Time to Elsa	64
Elsa Explains Time to Albert	65
Einstein Thinks About the Daughter He Put Up for Adoption and Then Could Never Find	66
Newton's Sailor	67
The First X-Ray, December 22, 1895	68
Aqueduct	69
Madame Curie	70
Seven Letters Written by Marie Curie to Pierre Curie After His Death	71
Caroline Herschel Discovers Her First Comet, Herschel C/1786 II P1	80

from The Next Stranger

House of Angels   89
With Suzanne   91
My Young Widow   93
The Awakening   94
On the Docks   96
Travelers   97
"Después de ahogado el niño, tapan el pozo"   98
Lady of the Haystack   99
A Fisherman Loves Sylvia   101

New &
Selected Poems

New Poems

Iceman

In bed
you lie with your back to me
and it is a lake of ice.
Like fish frozen under the cold,
frozen as they swam
(dead, but not dead, in a winter sleep),
I can see,
under the ice surface of your back,
the glimmer and blue and red
of spleen and kidneys,
the long pole of esophagus
under the frozen surface.

I place my hand on
your cold, cold skin
and crack the ice.
My hands enter you.

I can see my left hand
lightly hold your liver
and my right hand caress your ribs and then slide
down
the length of your arm
until your arm is a sleeve I am wearing
and my fingers rinse themselves in your fingers.

I want to dip my face into the lake of your back
and feel your vertebrae
like stones, uneven stones, on my cheek.
Can I open my eyes
under blood?

I push closer, take a deep mouthful of air,
and dive into your body.
With long strokes I move,
washing myself in you.
I swim down your leg
along the soleus muscle,
down past fibula, femur, down along the femoral vein
and down down down
under your heel—
where you touch ground.
I need to know how deep you are
how long my breath can last.

The Dream

In a glass dress everyone can see inside her body. If she wears a glass dress she has to walk carefully so that she doesn't fall and break her garment into pieces. A shard, splinter, or sliver of the glass dress can cut her arm. Under the glass dress, which surrounds the poet like a fish tank, I can see her navel float in the centre of the Earth. The sun shines through and flesh turns into water. I can see who places his hand under her dress. Through the glass dress, which surrounds the poet like a terrarium, at certain times I can see where the heart beats and where salamanders and horned toads hide. The man who loves her carves his initials in the glass with a Swiss army knife. A branch leaves scratch marks along the windowpane of her sleeve. She did not wear a glass slipper; she wore a glass dress.

Deus Ex Machina

For Reverend Martha Black Jordan

Because it rained inside the house
and became a house of tears
there were plastic buckets
and pans and pots and porcelain teacups
scattered everywhere filling with water.
Thimbles were set out to catch
the smallest drops.
I heard the sound of rain
or the sound of crying
and everything
—even the apples and figs—
tasted like salt.
One day I asked,
as I stood knee deep in water
in the middle of my bedroom,
"Is this a tragedy, this house?"
Sunday morning,
at the moment when my bed
began to float like a raft,
the great red tractor
drove up to my door with its headlights on
illuminating the Christian day.
As though it were bringing fire,

smoke poured out of its exhaust stack
and the sound of the potent diesel motor was thunder.
God drove the giant machine
that came to rib and plant
and harvest and rake
the wet, graveyard
earth of my house.

Scarecrow

When I see you at the end
of the cornfield
I still my breath.
you are so tall tied upright,
up high on a pole.
I have to lift my head to see you—
man of straw and rag—
and almost see your black Waterman-ink eyes
under the frayed Panama hat.
I know there is a 19-centimeter
Phoenix Sheath knife
with a black leather handle
and an engraved pommel and hilt
in the dishtowel
and mop padding at your waist.
I know there is a Colt .45 in dry grasses,
and, your favourite weapon,
a crowbar for a crow
in your sleeve.
Standing here, in the afternoon light
under your long Hitchcock-movie shadow,
my crow-heart
my crow-feather black,
crow-black crow heart

is scared of you,
scarecrow.
And even birds close their eyes.

Making Love in Spanish

When I make love to you in English
the objects in the room have no gender
and I only hear our voices.
But when I make love to you in Spanish
the chairs—those little girls—chatter,
and our shoes
want to step, with adoration, on the body
of light, lamplight,
that falls across the floor.
In Spanish the tangled sleeves of our sweaters
sigh with soft womanly voices,
and fall like long vines
around an armchair
that has become their master.
The roses bathe and bow
filled with desire for the clock
and the fragile windows
want to break into the mirror.
Here, your pockets worship
my stockings.
Here, the white walls worship
the white moon.
In the dark,
I give you my feminine mouth.
In the dark,
I give you my masculine eyes.

Swimming

In blue and sunlight,
in the lane beside my lane,
the wide arc of his arm
lifts and falls and covers my back
with a shower of water
so I swim in the rain.
As I finish lap number 24
I think that, under this spray,
we breathe the same air,
break the same water,
and we do not know each others' names.
Behind our goggles and plastic caps
we are the most beautiful people in the world
we are the most ugly people in the world.
For one kilometer,
through chlorine, bromine, and salt,
for the eternity of 30 minutes
we are married
in a swimming pool
that leads us, stroke by stroke,
to that beach.

The Ocean House

He built a house for me on the ocean floor
and planted a pine tree and azaleas.
He even built a chimney in the water—
a chimney I can swim up and down inside.
When I live in our ocean house,
I am not interested in rivers
and streams or even drinking water.

On the ocean floor,
when he says kneel, I obey.
The sun is obedient to the shadow.
The clouds are obedient to the wind.
My breath is obedient to my heart.
So when he asks
I kneel down on the sand
and rest my head against his knees.

In our ocean house the bricks sink
and the wooden beams float away.
Our clothes (and this is the truth)
are devoured by sharks
and a barracuda has eaten all his hats.
But he does not mind
and I do not mind

because, underwater,
we move so, so slowly
one dance can last for days.

The Night House

Here, to be truthful,
there are no hangers for my arms,

drawers for my legs,
hooks for my hands.

At night in the Night House
there is no shelf for my shadow.

Here, I go to sleep
with my body on.

I Wrote it for You

Here
take it in your hand
but don't hold it in a fist
or you'll crush the B's and T's,
the commas will fall out,
words will break into syllables
and the word "stiletto" become "let"
and the word "bayonet" become "bay".

If you read
between the lines
you'll find ankles and elbows
and the length of my back
like a slender strip of armour.
You'll find arms like spears
and chain mail
and gauntlet-covered hands.

A crossbow rests in a stanza break.

Carry this poem carefully,
cup it in your hands like you cup
your hands to carry sand,
so the words don't spill out

so you do not lose a single word,
or two words,
or the words:
I am your soldier.

Heart Poem

I place my hand
over your heart and your heart beats
in the 19th century.
I place my ear
on your heart
and listen and listen and listen
to the life of a man
who sounds like hail on cobblestones.

If we lie against each other
our hearts pressed together
I feel the pulse
of a man who loves me.

But late at night when you sleep—
and I am not so close—
I can still hear
the motor churn your body
across this lake of sleep
and it is more ancient.
Your heart, at the top of the Sun Pyramid,
once beat outside your body
for the sun.

How old are we?

This morning
I listen to myself,
afraid of the past that is coming.
In another century
I lost the pearl necklace
you gave me.
I am so sorry.

Do you remember so long ago?
I asked you then: Does your body belong to you
or does your body belong to God?

And do you remember when I placed a large glass
marble in your pocket?
You said it was the world.

Sometimes I don't know whose heart I hear.
Is it mine or yours?
If I rest my head against my arm
I can hear my heart in my sleeve.
Or is it you beating as you hold my hand?

In four days I will tell you the truth,
I promise.
Last winter
you lost me in the forest forever
and ever.

How old are we, really?

I remember the day you were born,
the medicines you took to heal
your childhood sicknesses,
and how you grew,
the glasses of milk you drank,

in order to stand here at the door
to await the new century.
I am beside you
in my blue gown
forever.

400 years ago
you were so frightened
when you were killed on a narrow road—
it was a dagger
straight through your heart.
I had to, my darling, comfort you
for hours.

Woodsman

for Ruth Fainlight

On page 4,
The woodsman did not kill Snow White.
He bent his bow
and, with a perfect mark,
he killed a deer.

On page 8 he said to the queen,
"Here is her almost-child,
almost-animal heart,
still warm,
even now filled with blood."

On page 12 the queen
spoke to her mirror.

What happened to the woodsman
after I closed the book?

He walked into the dark
forest of words,
letters like trees,
and lifted his axe.

Lady of the Broom

"There is a circumstance in his (Michael Johnson's) life some-what romantick, but so well authenticated, that I shall not omit it. A young women of Leek, in Straffordshire, while he served his apprenticeship there, conceived a violent passion for him; and though it met with no favourable return, followed him to Lichfield, where she took lodgings opposite to the house in which he lived, and indulged her hopeless flame. When he was informed that it so preyed upon her mind that her life was in danger, he with a generous humanity went to her and offered to marry her, but it was then too late; her vital power was exhausted; and she actually exhibited one of the rare instances of dying for love. She was buried in the cathedral of Lichfield; and he, with tender regard, placed a stone over her grave with this inscription:

Here lies the body of
Mrs Elizabeth Blaney, a stranger.
She departed this life
20 of September, 1694"

(from *The Life of Samuel Johnson* by James Boswell.)

I.

I call myself
Elizabeth.
My name means, "Consecrated to God",
and not "Wise Counsellor",
"Gazelle", or "Branch".
I descend the stairs
with overcast face,
barren mouth,
hair like a brat covers my head.
In the glade of my neck
there is heat.
I say my house has clean
water.
I open my hand to show
I do not carry a weapon.

II.

Strange to the morning,
foreign and unfamiliar to the evening,
this face is faceless,
a sea that wants to be
the ocean.

III.

How light my body feels,
how sure I am
that my arms can carry me.
I can live under trees
keep warm in papers and tatters,
and we will grow
against each other.
I count my fingers
they taste like grass. This happens
to those without shelter.

IV.

This is a covenant.
Come near.
Here I place my shoes,
a stone, wheat,
two sticks,
two words,
and this heap
I will name,
"everything is found."
Place your hand
beneath my thigh.

V.

The first time I looked at you
I could see my ancestors
in your face. My kin
peopled your eyes.
I knew then I would follow
your ways, my step
stepping in the dark step
of your shadow.
You never looked at me.
I know I am rough-hewn
and small.

VI.

I think of nests.
I think of the nest of the robin,
of the crested swallow
and can see myself
throwing sheets out of windows,
hanging towels
in the sun that finds them,
in the breeze that lifts them.
I will place two eggs in a basket
and wash and wash.
It is April
and the new , sudden rain
softens the ground.
The horseshoe is above the door,
the wheat in a bowl,
and I will plant roses in the house
I do not have.

I want to be in the mossy
air of garden gloves,
my hip against the heat
of a warm oven
I do not have.

VII.

My body heat is still inside
the sweater's sleeves,
a phantom body
of legs and hips in the skirt
are folded over a chair.
These clothes where I belong
protect my skin
from wind and sun
and skin of others.

VIII.

My dresses want to move
and cross their arms,
lift themselves up,
walk.

IX.

Beneath the bluff,
two miles from Leek,
a dead man was found.
Everyone went to see
his Jack-O-lantern face
cracked open,
skull with small hole
dipped into by bird.
Everyone said it was an ancient grave.

He lay with flint arrows
and one spear.
With spades and hoes and sharp rocks
they pulled him out and found
the secret tattoos:
blue cross behind his knee,
blue flower inked on ankle.

There, in his smallest piece of flesh,
were the shapes of ant hills,
wasp hives ,
colours of blue
bottle flies,
the sounds of summer.

I studied his hands,
his ribs,
and seams.

The bones of his spine
lay on the ground like a ladder.
I wanted to walk along those
bleached stepping-stones.
I thought he was my cousin.

X.

My dress,
and a chequered apron,
blew off the clothesline
into the trees.

All that my body once filled
and belonged to
you will find.
Once you also waked
without my head
on your arm,
my face in your hands,
my hands in your sleeves.

I feel my legs inside your legs
when you walk, walk, walk.

XI.

I will be your servant,
your Lady of the Broom,
and sow your shoes in pairs,
brush lint from your coat,
groom your house, cut,
harrow, rake, and weed the garden.
I will spit on the stain of your sleeve
and rub it clean,
spit on your silverware
to keep it bright.
Spit, spit, spit
and kiss the closed door
of the room where you read.

XII.

I am imperfect metal.
I am tin and lead that wants to be silver
or gold.
There is arithmetic in my house.
I count one and one is two.
I buy two pairs of black
gloves, two spoons,
two dresses, two of everything.
In my room
I have two chairs.
And the man who will love me,
will tell me
he has two arms.

XIII.

Along the water spine
of the river
there are so many broken
glass bottles
the shallow waves chime.

XIV.

You did not know.
You have always been growing
toward me: learning to walk,
to pronounce the letter "T",

taking medicine,
knowing your name.
Every step you climbed
was taking you here
to stand
beneath me
or above.

XV.

The sound of my broom
brought you here
and my empty skirts
stretched out on the line
in the sun, in the wind,
clapping together like flags.

You watch from across the wall
and learn the way I stir.

You want to pull
this blouse off
my shoulders.

You want to sleep
with your arms
in my sleeves.

XVI.

I miss you even
            when you are here.

XVII.

Close your eyes because it will be
as if you are not here.

The sea travels in my blood
and wants to be the ocean.
I've thought of this before.

XVIII.

Warm my hands.
I am cold.

Fingers link like a net
To draw you in.
I am a garment,
you can wear me and button
me at your wrists,
line your clothes with my body.

I listen to you. I build
a steeple with my hands.

I look in your eyes
and miss your mouth.
I touch your hand
and miss your fist.
When we walk I hear your footsteps
and miss your voice.
When I stand beside you
I want to be carried.

XIX.

I dream about a round room—
corners afflict me,
"Sit in the corner until the cock cries,
cock-a doodle-do." my father used to say.

Because I never knew you,
smelled your skin, farmed you,
elbowed my way up your side,
I drink too much water.

I know the rabbit meat is under-cooked,
the potatoes are green,
the plum jelly is too black.

I have tried some remedies:
My pillow cases were rubbed
on silver.
My cups and spoons were filled with salt.
My lips were painted with beetroot.

Who decided that I should live or die?

Father,
I have not seen my face in someone's eyes.
No one has ever said, "there, there…"

I remember when they slit the deer's belly
and the foetus lay furless
but with small hooves formed.
The hunters clapped, bit their thumbs,
and slapped their thighs.
"Counts as two!"
"This is a good omen."
"Don't whine girl, be a man, be a prince."
"The hunt was ripe!"

Without a mother,
no girl walks safely,
no other will place their body
between her body
and the bear.

XX.

The seamstress measures
my waist: 22 inches. Measures
my thigh and wrist.
Length of neck: 5 inches.
Weight: 9 stone.

A Cobbler measures my feet.
Left: 6 inches. Right: 5 inches.
I give them a sack filled with onions.

The surgeon cannot stop my nose bleed.
Turnips and beetroots

are placed beneath the pillow.
My hair is washed, my hands are washed.
One of my squirrels dies. Yes,
I want to keep its fur.

My mother once told me,
"Your first breath, birth-breath,
smelled like the river and dry grass."
I cup hands around my mouth
to smell the young breath
of river, dry grass, milk.
Smell of acorn and wool,
smell of carpet and dog.

…a dim and thistled dawn,
too silent for rising. Two dresses stand
in my room on poles. Two
pairs of shoes by my bed.
In the very last prune-dark minutes—
where no bird sound breaks—
I can feel the light
returning to the stars. It is too quiet yet
for prayers.

XXI.

There are the shapes of people in the air.
A hand moves through bower and thistle,
arms alter the swell along brick and tile,
someone walks in orbit.
See the cloud shaped like my dress,
rain falls through the fold and lint. This minute
while I am breathing

a sailor blows out a candle.
Some things I have seen
were not asked for.
We walk in the organ grinders' footsteps.

There is no pitter-patter in the breeze that blows
the whisper of our voices through the air
following other words that are misshapen and mixed
where alphabet becomes geography.
Other words move around the house,
into cups.

I write in the air as I walk
with the penmanship of my body.

XXII.

Your words in the air
blow into my blouse.

XXIII.

Dream:
I mend my clothes
while wearing them. I turn up
the hem of my dress
and fix it with thread.
It is like stitching sorrow to your back.
In the dream I also sew on a button
while wearing my robe.

"If you mend clothes on your back
you'll have to wear black."
When I had something new
from the seamstress,
she'd say, "Health to wear it,
strength to tear it,
and money to buy another."

Sometimes I wear my clothes
inside out. This is lucky.
Sometimes I rent my garments
to know I am still strong.

XXIV.

This is not the house that Jack built,
nor the crooked house with a crooked fence,
this is the house of a wife, a cook,
a mop and a pail.
Nailed to the wall,
this is not a star
but bent and brittle branches—
the dry skeleton
of a kite.
This is not a swallow
but a small clipped hawk
step, step, stepping under
the willow's shade.
And this, this is not a goldfish but a black
spotted salamander,
gills against glass
where there is no reef
or stone.

XXV.

I have always known you
    and you are what I have found.
Before you were born
    you called to me for water.

XXVI.

I need the medicine of metals:
Lunar caustic, vitriol of Venus, and sugar of Saturn.
The alchemist tells me I am missing sulphur
in my skin. He tells me to eat salt.
He tells me I am a pelican
with blood on my breast.
He even asks me, asks me twice,
why I am so alone.
"Why, Mistress, why?"

The salt makes me so thirsty
I can taste the centre of the Earth.

XXVII.

An anchor with
arm, crown, throat and palm,
falls for shallows,
falls for shoals.

Only water reflects blue.
The sea is always
darker or lighter blue,
and water in my drinking glass is lightest.

XXVIII.

Be quiet.
Be quiet.

There is a package wrapped
in brown paper and tied with string. I steal
things that belong to him. I stole his sweater and scarf.
When I die
he will open my packages and find his own belongings.
He will never tell anyone.
He is a gentleman.
He knows how to keep
quiet.

XXIX.

This was written
so you would not hear a sound.

XXX.

Peeling apples.
This afternoon,
while slicing the bruised apples,
I thought, we need to know each other
carefully. The sun dazzles
on my kitchen knife.

XXXI.

Tonight you think you sleep with me.
What sweet animal lies in your blankets?
Fawn or rabbit?
It moves to the right,
sleeps on its right side,
warm fur against your legs.
It is so like me
we cast one shadow.

XXXII.

Another dream:
I saw my skeleton
and there were marks along my bones.
Some people were said,
she has arms for pushing wheelbarrows,
she is a woman who never left the cave,
or feared fire.

XXXIII.

Drink my tears.
You can smell the lame animal.
I could poison you with my body.

XXXIV.

I am homesick when I'm home.
I miss the chair I sit in. I long
for the dress I am wearing.
The first time I saw you
I wanted to see you. The first time I touched
your arm I wanted to touch your arm.

I thought, "I wish he were sick."
I wish you had a fever so I could care for you.

"If he were lame
he'd have to lean on me."

XXXV.

You are a man who loves books and parchment.
You read Petrarch, Anacreon, Hesiod,
and your hands smell like sheepskin.
With ink and quill I write
a word on my stomach.

XXXVI.

In Lichfield,
down the street from the apothecary
there lives a collector.
He has boxes filled with berries
that have turned to stone,
stones, clay jars,
jars filled with dried onion skins,
goatskins, sheepskins, deerskins
piled one against the other,
and other hidden things in dark bottles.
When I walk past his house,
the air is frost-bitten.

At the apothecary
I buy chervil and nightshade to soothe
my throat. I speak your name
too often. The letter "M" is the 13th letter
of the alphabet. I must voice you in my mind
and not in my mouth.

Along the road, lying on the cobbled stones,
there is a black wool coat. Once there was a boot,
once there was a glove.
Many things have been lost.
I still have my belongings. I miss
what I have.

XXXVII.

Thinking of my dowry.
This is what I own:
two hats,
three dresses,
a skirt and two blouses,
one petticoat,
two pairs of gloves,
two pairs of shoes,
one large sheepskin bag,
one book of psalms,
four hair pins,
two legs,
two eyes,
feet and hands and blood,
my name, two arms that open
and close, open and close, open and close.
My reaper's voice,
threshing vowels and consonants:
A, B, C.

XXXVIII.

I know how to tie
sheepshank rope knots,
figure-eight knots,
and bowline knots
with my eyes closed.

With my eyes closed
I can knit, cook, and walk
to the corner,
and cathedral.

If I close my eyes
you cannot see me.

XXXIX.

Last night I practised divinations.
I rubbed amber on my wrist,
near the instep,
on the throne
of my heart.
I burned a broom in the fire
and read the blue and red sparkle,
counted the flames.
Nobody has heard me today.
There was a bird in my house.

XL.

I wish I had a sword,
to be buried with a sword.
Bury me with a thimble.

XLI.

I have read *Astrologaster*, *The Living Library*,
Secret Miracles of Nature,
and other books.

I have read, "If a candle burn blue,
it is a sign there is a spirit in the house,
or not far from it."

And, "Coral bound to the neck
takes off turbulent dreams,
and allays the nightly fears of children."

And, "Whether there be any magic in the practice
of some young women too curious,
who upon Allhallow eve go to bed
without speaking to any,
having first eaten a cake made of soot,
and dreaming, see in their sleep,
the man that shall be their husband."

And, "An opinion there is,
which magnifies the condition
of the fourth finger of the left hand;
presuming there is a cordial relation,
that a … nerve, vein, or artery,
is conferred thereto from the heart,
and therefore that especially hath the honour
to bear our rings."

From these pages I have learned
it is unlucky to sweep a table with a broom,
lend my soap, cross my fingers in church,
or say prayers backwards. I have never said,
"Name thy be hallowed
Heaven in art who father our."

XLII.

After Michaelmas
I have never
worn my apron outside
under the clouds. I have never walked
backward
through a door,
or slept on my left side. I have never
let scissors fall from my hands.
I have never spoken about you.

XLIII.

The chemist says I have night-blindness.
I cannot see the nut-pick, nutcracker,
pan or pail. I drink a fluidram of
raisin water,
a fluidounce of prune water,
and wash my eyes with apple vinegar.
If I could see,
I would find my way.

XLIV.

I have followed you
for miles. I know the sound
of your footsteps,
the twist and clap
of your boot on stone.

I have wanted to lie down
so you could walk
over my body.

XLV.

If I am found,
I will be found on a bridge.
Some people may say
I was troubled in mind,
that I possessed a vile
and venomous melancholy.
I only needed a sister.

XLVI.

I sit outside
your door on the slate-blue step
and hear you
inside
move and breathe and blow
out the candle.

Inside or outside,
it is still the same night.

XLVII.

This is what happened:

A spirit
lives in me
in a place between the apple
and the apple skin, a place
between sleep and morning,
between my skin and blood.
He is black
and white, polished and dangerous
as a domino.
The beat of his boots is in my voice,
the blow of his boots is in my voice.
Yoked to my waist,
he whispers with a noise of hooves
and wagon wheels. At daybreak,
I comb tangle and snarl from my hair,
wet my eyes, wash my eyes.
Even though I knot my fingers,
tie them together,
he still holds my hands.

XLVIII.

When I am sick with broken pulse,
you cross the street, enter my house
and the air is laden with the scent of books:
a tang of cotton thread, ink, and bark.

I hear you say, "this is the beginning."
"You will be well."

"I will buy you bride cake, a new broom,
wedding plates."

Under your shade,
I can speak. There are promises in my mouth:
"I will be your Lady of the Cleaver,
Lady of the Pencil,
Lady of the Shears,
Lady of the Shell, Swan, and Stick.
I will be your marrow.
I will take your name."

from Newton's Sailor

Far from the Smoked Glass*

With his sweater inside out,
in the closed light of the room,
far from the smoked glass,
far from the domino numbers
and wooden telescopes,
Einstein waited.
He stirred the tea bright
and as mid-day
drew the dark,
as African stars pulled
out of orbit
—at the young
eclipsed minute—
he felt the soft
lamplight
bend around his shoulder
like an arm.

* In 1919, photographs taken of a solar eclipse in Africa
confirmed Einstein's Theory of Relativity.

Einstein Explains Time to Elsa

We are seventy
we are sixteen.
Here you feed me oranges,
even in winter,
here the flowers live
as you cut them,
here you lift up your skirt
again and again and again.
And the air inside
our hands is for breathing
and the sand,
within the hourglass,
always falls
for the sea.

Elsa Explains Time to Albert

I went to the butcher shop
and I must have brushed
up against something
there is blood on my skirt.

At first I thought
I've cut myself,
I've cut myself many times.
Calf blood or rabbit blood?

I don't know.
When did it live?
Is it still alive?
Where is it learning to sleep?

I must put my skirt
in cold water. I know
it will always have blood on it
even if I turn off the light.

Einstein Thinks About the Daughter He Put Up for Adoption and Then Could Never Find

Perhaps.
She uses her fingers
like a compass
making circles in the dirt.

Perhaps
she cuts her hand
in the dark day,
splitting an atom
in the middle of her palm.

Particles of light curve
through glass-empty windows.

Numbers tattooed on her wrist
are blue equations,
and the knots in the barbed wire
look like stars.

He hugs his violin,
small body of wood.

Newton's Sailor

Sprung from rope and rust and ocean duff,
custodian of bladed corals
and one wood compass,
mariner of all movement
he navigates his ship,
navigates the pale liquid
that furls to tides,
a planet that wheels the sun.

Listen to the pitch of his step:
One, two, three, four, five.
Some nights no sleep returns,
One, two, three, four, five,
across the voyage of the deck.

And this helmsman,
who drinks sour malt
and reads the clouds,
can never stop the velocity.
No matter how far he pulls
his breath, stills
and surrenders the sail,
he can never make port.

The First X-Ray, December 22, 1895

It was his wife's left hand,
a skeleton on the photographic plate
slim as silverware.
In that claw of cartilage and bone
he saw the shadow of a ring
on her fourth finger,
he saw her grave.

Aqueduct

He spits saliva into his hand
and cleans my face.

At night we smell
the aqueduct,

and two dungeon trees.
In the morning, early,

I swim
in the stone

and, for the first time,
open my eyes

under water.

Madame Curie

Since the rains began
you have become more feverish,
Mistress Skeleton.

You say, "Take the black sea
urchin off the black piano,
my hands are too burned,"
and wonder at the length
of your tibia.

Only some know of the birthmark,
shaped like a hoof,
on the left side
of your waist. Only a witch
can turn white
into red—they say.

Inside glass cylinders you find
the milk light,
heat in stones.
You are too slim today,
scented in radium salts and blue,
to carry the rings on your fingers.

Seven Letters Written
by Marie Curie to Pierre Curie
After His Death

Letter I

Kindled by uranium
the great room glowed.
Even from two streets away,
as we walked to the laboratory,
We could see the matter
Through the window's seams.
Inside, your chair and lab coat
grew sheer, green, phosphorescent,
pencils were luminous.
Albino rays appeared
in the decimals of our cells
as we quietly became radioactive.
You said, "polonium, radium",
and your tongue and teeth were yolk opalescent
as if your speech were lit.
I wrote, " I extracted from the mineral
the radium-bearing barium and this,
in the state of chloride,
I submitted to fractional crystallization,"
and the paper warmed
to 98.9 degrees Fahrenheit.
In that room,
black and white
had left the world.

Letter II

The wheel of the wagon crushed Pierre Curie's skull,
killing him instantly.

Where are you?
Where the wheel is a wing?
Dragonfly wing,
hawk wing or angel wing?

I feel the wing in my body,
wing in my radius and ulna bones,
      sleek geometry
        of fin and feather.

I stretch out my arms,
I stretch out my arms.

Letter III

Dear Pierre,

Whom I will never more see here,
I want to speak to you
In the silence of this laboratory,
Where I never thought I would have to live
without you."

Today, there is not a living thing
in this laboratory.
No voice.
No movement.
No hum or furnace.

There are vats filled with pitchblende,
test tubes, pans, weights, scales,
this quiet, thermometer, protractor,
rulers, glass slides,
microscope and this quiet
of angles and barium
on a plate, sliced crystals
and quiet Polish ore.
I need you in the structured
heraldry of this place.

In 1901 you tested the burn,
placed barium on your arm for ten hours.
We kept a log:
Day 4: Burn: darker.
Day 15: No change.
Day 20: A scab appeared.
Day 23: Open wound.
Day 34: No change.
Day 52: Small, dark oval.
Day 62: No change.

Pale and parched we stood
collars open, shoes unlaced.
Our fingers were too burned to dress.
We carried instruments in our teeth
and touched each other with our wrists.
Quietly, you told me, "All the laboratory
animals have died".

We spoke the verbs to add, to ask.
I asked if the barium had been measured yet.
I asked if you were hungry.
I asked if the fraction met
yesterday's result.

Subtract, divide, add and multiply
are words of faith.
3 is yellow, 2 is quiet,
0 is a cell, is a moon, is a mouth,
The number 5,
with its severe geometry,
holds me still.
There is heat and history in numbers.
I have kept your death from the equations
in case they lose courage.

Letter IV

Take. Take the rain
tenderness around the grey, still fern.
Between September and next year,
fragments of Autumn
appear and dwell in peat—
light is at the edge of my hands...

                                          I dream you:
we read:
A child was found in the mountains
choked by a butterfly.
The wings, antennae and fragments of pollen still
lay in the throat.
Then you said,
"A leaf has a backbone,
A feather has a backbone
A fish has a backbone."

Today I wish my name were, "Ruth".
I would bring you barley
where you lodge I will lodge.
Blue of a crow's feather evening rain
I touch the space
where you have been.

Letter V

Moon of ailments, moon
in this envelope, moon on shale
and blue wall,
balm over hands stitching
buttons back. Look in the jam jar
of all the misplaced buttons find
the white shell-thin
one with four eyes. For this all
am I grateful. I can sew
the sliver out of your sleeve,
brush the light
off your clothes with boar bristles.
Scythe to the sudden joy—
my arm has opened.

Letter VI

the ash tree will die
I told them to cut it
for the shade
pretended to be asleep
so many nights you
we were radium-weary blue
quiet with questions and
I walk backward now toward
they tell me I never finish
sentences whisper so call it
pitchblende poison
living without your eyes open
closed open if you looked
away from me
I was jealous even
of statues

Letter VII

I am the woman without gloves.
I sift soil instead of flour.
I am a gardener.
I search for the black star
and white crow.
Soil on my apron and neck
soil in my eyes.
Remember, remember everything
we found as we worked:
a fork, yellow hair, brown hair, squirrel bones...
how well we knew the earth
you lie in.
I wash and bathe and wash
and feel the water's skin.

Caroline Herschel Discovers Her First Comet, Herschel C/1786 II P1

I

I saw blue coma, nucleus,
head and dust,
heard the gravelled wind,
the race of stones.

I have studied the threshold
of horizon,
sutured brink
where ships used to fall over
the Earth's edge forever.
Now the sailors always return,
now the sailors always return.

II

"It's dusk," I say this everyday.
William says, "Let's stand
beneath the oak."
We plough the night between
Winter and October. He finds the things
I almost see.

III

My locket has no child's face.
My locket has my own hair
pleated there.

IV

William is away.
I brighten the silver,
and notice the chairs
don't hold me in the same way and everything
leans a little away from its place.
Apples lie above the plums.

V

I listen for the whistle of arrow and flint, listen,
place lavender leaves in my blouse,
wax the telescope.
Sometimes, I pray:

Night, night, night in heaven
let it be known that a woman came
into the sky
I am servant.
The light of the body is the eye.

VI

Unroll the rolled-up map
weight the corners
down with candlesticks
sharpen the graphite
and draw the space-filled triangle
(the black between stars)
measure, subtract, divide
at 42 degrees I see a shadow—
only light can make a shadow.

VII

That was when
take me, take me
there was no one to take me
arm-wrapped, sister
against some quiet name.
I take myself to the window,
"Look," I say. An orb of stone
has fallen in the garden.

VIII

I also have a spade
for what is soft and close and yields
to me.

IX

All is borrowed:
stone in the drawer,
my hand in the crook of cup,
figs that are too young
to crystallize.
Many times and more
I hold the stone in my palm
like a thief.

X

There are no clouds. The night has exhaled
to me. The sky is in the telescope, the comet
has coursed into my eye, into the black
sky of my pupil,
its grit and grain teeth and plume all.

I am owl in flight
with grey warm
rabbit in my claws.

I place my right hand
in my left glove
and cover the telescope
with my shawl
to keep it warm.

from The Next Stranger

House of Angels

for Barbara

After the supermarket,
in the steel elevator light,
I watch the silence of my sister's
face in profile
brushing her tears upward
as if to put them back inside—
weary of these paper bags,
these concrete homes in the sky.

We feel, sometimes, so ready for sleep,
thinking of the night
fish markets, remains of what we were.
So ready for sleep,
while red snappers are being laid out
beside open barrels of squid and crab
claws in wire cages
press out
        out of wire.

We long for a backward country,
to be the wives of fishermen,
to step inside ancient steps.
And among fossiled shells,

shark's teeth, coral seeds,
hunt
the lost bones of our faces.

With Suzanne

Dressed in black lace and red lipstick,
and Suzanne looking just like Minnie Mouse,
we'd walk past Houston Street
to get her drugs
and then back to her apartment
that smelled of prunes and oil paint
where she'd written,
"She makes hungry, where most she satisfies,"
on the wall above her bed.

We would listen to Peggy Lee sing *Fever*
and drink gold apple juice
from a refrigerator covered
in Basquiat's doodles—(one day
she'd sell it at Christies
for five thousand dollars.)
Suzanne says she found Jean-Michel
on a bench in Washington Square Park.

Another one she lost and loved
was Michael Stewart
killed by seven policemen
for painting graffiti in a subway station.
I call her "widow".

She can talk and talk about her stray, small dark boys
who touched the night in her hair.

Her hands rarely open
but stay curled in small fists,
hiding phone numbers
written in black ink along her fingers.
Some of her clothes
she's never washed
because they still carry the scent
of some evening.

When Suzanne cleans out her closets
she gives me these clothes—
sweaters that no longer matter
from affairs that have passed,
but still smell of wine
and keep me dressed
in other people's kisses.

My Young Widow

Suzanne lives only in corners,
cloaked in her bat-black cloth
she smells of convent walls.
She has a Rembrandt-pallor,
spook eyes,
and smiles
the secret, half-smiles
of nuns.

On spider-quiet evenings,
Suzanne's breath
is filled with candles,
as her magic-lantern eyes
seek him still.
And in her hummingbird-voice,
voice of a sleepwalker,
she calls to her lost husband.
There are no teeth
inside her words.

The Awakening

Late one summer night
the pirate visited me.
I showed him
the hem of my skirt
and how to put on my rings,
I let him wash my face
and cut my hair.

From his ship
he brought seawater for me to drink,
and he made me put out the candles
with my hands
to burn them.
He told me to give him everything
that belonged to me.

So I gave
my boxes of needles and threads,
my green velvet dress,
books closed
and filled with my breath.

All afternoon,
as the sun burns my cheeks
I feel him behind me

walking on the bones
of my shadow.

On the Docks

Sheltered inside my own
vaporous breath
of syrup, sun and clay
I feel darker
than my own shadow.
All within me waits for him
as I suck on a pomegranate,
the only fruit
that has teeth.

Travelers

for Captain George N. Sibley

We need the unknown landscape
where the moon is hunted,
hunted like a jaguar, bear and squirrel,
and the night is arrow-poisoned
black with curare.
Songs sound like rain,
fish swim the air
and comets,
mercury-tailed comets,
rip open the sky
and scatter moon-stones, silver ash
and the wail of a million
insect wings. We are
forever moving,
full of an opal-lust,
toward the next taste
of flower with salt,
the next strange touch
of ivory, black pearl and perfect
fossiled sea horse
lying in our palms. Forever moving,
we share
the acrobat's soul
who like all stars
seek the falling.

"Después de ahogado el niño, tapan el pozo"*

White-ghost centipedes, larvae,
tadpoles, gravel,
shards of brick, blue moss,
spit and coins,
slab of wood,
sodden jacaranda leaves,
swallow feather,
beetle wing, reflected moon
and one small shoe.
All covered now
by metal sheets
and piles of stone.
But the dark well water
seeps through the ground
under dirt roads
and into the crops and gardens.

* *Mexican saying: "After the child drowns, they cover the well".*

Lady of the Haystack*

Strange abacist,
she'd count pebbles and count
the flecks, specs and particles
of her grass nursery.
She knew all
that dwelled in her damp berth,
thick with ants,
it was an atlas
of cobwebs, thistle-down,
the tiniest mushrooms
and weed.

On brumal, frosty nights,
through the yellow-mustard hay,
she'd add and subtract meteors,
comets, shooting stars,
blue fireflies,
and fill her twisted sorrow
with numbers.

And later, years later,
at the stark,
black-box asylum.
she'd count her strands of hair
and stand only by windows.

Still, her breath smelled grainy
of all the earth's dark sediments.
And all the other melancholy
madwomen
sheltered near her
for the sugar
sweet hay scent
of her arms.

* The Lady of the Haystack made her appearance in 1776 near Bristol.
She lived for four years in a haystack before being moved to an asylum.

A Fisherman Loves Sylvia

Sylvia's fisherman is jealous,
full of sulk and scowls,
jealous in his fist and teeth
because Sylvia of the Swans,
Sylvia of the Secret Eyes
sleeps.
Lulled and warm,
burrowed deep in quiet breath,
Sylvia's dreams steal her away
from his cave-dark,
briny shelter.
And he wants to be saved
from these night robberies,
wants to cocoon his nets
around her
and pierce the slim, red
feathered hooks
into her skin.

Printed in the USA
CPSIA information can be obtained
at www.ICGtesting.com
LVHW090107081223
765871LV00001B/79